TRESPASSING

Poems

Patrizia de Rachewiltz

UNO PRESS

Printed in the USA
Library of Congress Control Number: 2011926696
ISBN: 978-1-60801-060-8

Cover art: *Reflection* 2008 by Patrizia de Rachewiltz
Book Design: Carrie Chappell

unoPRESS
University of New Orleans Publishing

Managing Editor, Bill Lavender
www.unopress.org

The Ezra Pound Center for Literature

Trespassing is No. 2 in the Ezra Pound Center for Literature Book Series

Series Editor: John Gery, University of New Orleans

Table of Contents

IV. Trespassing

V. No Way Out

VI. Back to the Earth with Feathers

TRESPASSING

I. The Princess of Crumbs

The Princess of Crumbs

The house in the calle
held sixty people,
in the evening glow...
a Poet in the cusp of time,
old faces behind shutters
mesmerized.
Leaning against the warm wall,
we the keepers
of pomegranate sunsets.
The birds flew high, looping
circles
in the kindling light.
For the cravings of the heart,
a coming home,
as memories
dwindled away,
the calle empty of shadows,
gone,
the long figure with his cane.
And the princess
with leftover crumbs
in the small of her hand,
tiny morsels
to feed voracious dreams.

To Know You

Loose rocks
balanced—the green world,
my bare feet stinging on cold grit—
peeled off

my flesh from bone,
dead white.
I can be your ghost or shadow.

I can be a walking miracle,
my face flat
against the greenness of ferns,

my mind a rock,
a troll, in a million of filaments.
My arms shred the sky,
nursing it to stillness,

and I dig a small hole to bury myself
under a cross of twigs: here lies misery. Wind
grumbles,
cathedrals born on wind.

The taste of root,
of earth,
on cracked lips.
This way only can I say I know you,

the howling of a moon-hit wolf,
your fog-draped heart.
A beggar

with your worn leather pouch
tied at your waist,
your heavy foot on my mound
crushing

my lungs, hunger for bliss,
I forget—

seared to your flesh—
that misery is better than nothing.

Anonymous Venetian

The green, yet the green of you,
grows darker, stilled
blackberry dew and water.
The green breaks the surface

and the twilight screams:
The you, the green, the water.
Then the red, within the red, the deep
ripe juicy red of you.

Like sap of leaf it seeps through
your throat, old splendours
sealed in sirih red.
Hush, but hear and hear,

a slow regatta dyes the dark—
anonymous, liquefied time.
Your boat
a lantern for the dead lilacs,

and through all the air
the you, the winged, the feathered:
May we rise together—
we borrowers of deep scars.

Each Time I Move

through your walls I move
closer to your womb-webbed island,
the grind of color and bone rubbed down
to a line in the shore

Dim cool moons stream upwards
waiting, all the hours before spring
waiting
to tear apart
the warm cocoon husks around each other

in the limbo where fugitives turn

I light
green candles in the night
lacking eternity

The Other Woman

Radiant
as if granted a wish,
her white hands unfolding,
caught in the eerie light,
where whispers dwell in the corners
in the stillness
of her sanctuary,
she holds her face, unmasked,
her other self cupped in her hand.

The other woman takes her,
their eyes alike, their fingers locked.
Somewhere from the stilled air
come signs unveiled.
She is the wing, she the sound
from her golden bow.
Eyes wide open,
there is no other self than the purer side of her.

On My Knees

The light is green and soft:
I break from the dream
and separate the seed
from its tender stalk,
daring spring, by woman's touch,

to hold the wave of golden
hair against my face
and bring me to my knees
like a Muslim at dawn
against the sighing wall

until the silver moon calls again.

My Room

My room is full of wonders,
My mind full of webs.
The cocoon is stuck
Between two beams.
Then the miracle:
A sudden burst of colours
So that after the shedding
First comes bliss.

The Color of Pearl

Old with time
The curtains are as stitched and mended,
As my face,
No strength to pull them
Down and draw new patterns
On each stain.
When it rains they fill up like sails, carrying me onward.

The plant is
Luscious and glad. I bathe it in water
And milk
And the promise of a sunnier day.
I cannot grow
Lavender outside
My window; I have memories instead of a view.

I barely
Touch the surface.
Strong roots pull at my feet.
I know the bottom.
It is what you fear. I have known it, I do not fear it.
I catch its radiance
And hold out my hand—not to bend
Like a willow.

Shall I bring you
The sound of the wave?
It sleeps in me,
Feathery,
An abandoned cry
Looping and spiraling, melting
Slowly
Beyond the breakwater
as I wake and fight for air.

I am all washed out:
The color of pearl. Over the mirror
I hang sheets.
The night crackles with its bony face, while

The cat
Seeming to see,
Wishing to eat the green edges,
With its almond eyes contemplates the world.

Numinous Nightshade

High turrets in my dream
the poet of Salamanca
    in the sea-shelled house
Isabella de Castile's daughter
    Joana la loca
rode on her horse balanced
on one thigh
and I
fell over the cliff as my horse tripped
waking 300 years later
    into another life.
What are the ways of the wind?
The poisonous thorns
    a bee's sting
or the bite of a red brown copperhead?
"Miao" was their nickname
    three ancient coins
"bloody tears flow" (Confucius)
    Kên above
    K'AN below
One should not persist in this!
        A whiteness
more pure than cloud
to broaden the mind
    in a myriad of petals blooming.
Did you say 'love is dancing'?
If stranded on an island
would you eat me
  or shake coconut trees to feed me?
A strong pillared cathedral
  in Hieronymus bois le duc,
a fence around it to warn drunken men
from pissing in the corners.
   Home may not be a haven anymore,
knows the cat with yellow eyes
or the white rabbit on the balcony,
   concrete instead of a meadow
in the dream again
   swallowed by a pink-bellied trout

slowly, as the snake swallows its prey
craving a soliloquy,
to reach numinous grace
the tortuous twists of the mind,
the convoluted heart.
Tell me now, where is your promised temple?
I am still climbing...

II. Radiant Thresholds

Barbl, Who Knew Me

Hair snow-white, rosy
cheeks—
she held me
newborn,

when the castle doors
were still unhinged
and the wind
blew fierce—

proud of her old age,
with a small kerchief
balled
in her hand,

the same hand
that held me
once
on her tiny bosom.

Madrigal

For our father's fathers
and their antique spirits,
we travelled, facing each other,
to Salamanca.

Centuries of quiet alabaster
tear-tongued in my throat.
The running bull, the insulting fear.
But you looked on,
whereas I died, my ear cut off,
dragged by the tail from the crowds,
my life cut short
among the cheers.

How could I tell you
I left my ear in Salamanca?
Your laughter and your sneer
will follow me elsewhere,
and small by small
I'll lose my limbs.
The last to go
will be the chain around my neck
dug up centuries after
and in a log-book
neatly noted: date unclear.

Canto

You are the ring in the tree,
the shadowed brow, the hard resin.
From your lilied ancestry seeps the sap
as it grows, filled with the pomegranate.
Limpid tender root anchored in the lake,
braided hair in your sleep --
in one single bough of time
two boughs. The whim against blinds and beams
has given way to the night of the mountain.
Against you hurled an infrequent rival,
a succession of sunsets.

The Canto goes on consuming sky,
its vale of tears inherited.
Poets die prisoners
but not the dawn.
Tree trunk Brancusian becomes light
and the bird is looking for you.
Not many flowers I picked but oceans,
to me as, slender plumed swallow,
you gave way to wings and a solid perch.

At last the light diffuses my first wails,
and I listen to the sighing of the wind.
Transparent tree,
our home has radiant thresholds.
I seek beyond time and find there
peace,
as your voice sings to me.

Your Poem

Letter from my mother...
            my father moved through depths of light...
my father moved through grief and joy...

said e. e. cummings, now your poem
            has just arrived
to extend paradise.

Quieter Again

for my mother

You are quieter again, the valley
at your feet in the morning,
and the first bird darts
across your face.

Stone upon stone, piled up
the years of solid walls,
to split the strain
of many lives.

In the wind your melancholy
dances still, while
the cherry sap pours
through your fingers.

The vastness of sky in your eyes,
an infinite
succession of antique verses,
renews itself

in your soul, wrapped with care
by heedless winds
and the green of time. The cross
of roses

stands out on the slopes, as you return
to the womb where the slow
river speaks of the dear poet.
The cricket

looks out for you in summer sleep
to love you;
the strength of remembering
lies in starting all over.

The Beaches of Agami

for my father

Awakened by the myth of the angry god,
out on the shore you heard the sea call.

I see your footprints in the sand.
My bed was empty and now
you are running along the shore before light.

The Sea of Agami drowns women
for their sins.
You see me
coiled in the spiral, fragile,
even in something so fluid and green,
no god, no sacrifice to the angry sea.
You taught me how to please a man, that
is what a woman is for
and what moon more splendid,
what fragrance!
a light and a look at the growing—

My mind smiles in the mirror, the white
beaches have softened my skin,
and I kneel like a rabbit
and stretch my arms upward.
I might die and the softness go away
without my finding out what love is -

(From father to daughter, a gift.
The plane swayed towards Egypt.)

Ghosts

All night the ghosts spoke to me:
I roamed through the house on bare feet,
the night crushed against the panes,
faces white and glaring, spilling light,
singing, moaning, dancing slow dances.
Take me into your world, I asked,
I am not fit for living.
The cat watched me with green eyes.
She could see the dancers clearly,
maybe grey cats jumping in the air,
and babies stillborn.

No more corners in my heart,
no more thresholds,
nor patterns that can't be broken.
To be a fitting gift for those slow dancers
I make myself light, frigid and cold,
embracing the hollow air.
The despair entangled in my hair
may well then leave me, and the solitude
which I keep making
forsake its claws at my flexing jaws—

to be an angel before my time
with a crown of daisies and vines
between my toes, with the light
on my body set apart from the cold,
and not to be afraid anymore.

III. Day after Day

Another Dawn

Another way of praying,
autumn weary—with birds,
God's finger to his lips.
Still,
the quietness—
the governed soul grows
in the nine mansions of Avila,
a fountain built near its source.
Mirrored shards
wedged in her broken world:
One shard
is her birth mountain
saved by cross and grind,
expanding in honour and toil.
One shard
on a shore in a pharaoh's land,
a rifle to her head,
where a father was led
by her footprints in the sand
to the vortex
of the wave dying.
One shard
in an infant's throbbing little heart,
earth angels
in heaven's glow—
and one shard
in golden stone, 300 years before,
the bridle path too steep,
where she was left broken
in that deep ravine,
her last breath on her lover's lips—

The wound is open,
a bee making honey in the hive.
Her eyelids stir,
as she wakes into another dawn,
his arms still around her.

March '98

I was standing in front of a vast plane:
No tree, no bush, no sound. No bird.
All that came before now laid out for me.
Wet, shiny and smooth as from a lake.
Nor the time now nor after.

Never so clear, all on its own, now made fluid:
A solitary voyage. But without the mask.
It's harder now. It shouldn't be.
Thoughts are screened, subdued, and hushed...
Another silence born, a tremor.
Around me, winged, hover the little lights.

May

Tree in bloom:
    one by one
        the petals fall
in the small
    wind
        as I gaze
and remember
    not to suffer
        since time
made water
    always
        returns.

Meeting

When I meet you
it's no matter if
          I don't see
the edge of the sea.

Like a sailboat
my mind is
          always more at ease
in open waters...

June '98

the moon only slightly elliptic
therefore subject to no shame
therefore infinite...

From Sapphire Blue

Days endless bring voices as of ravens
coming down the valley onto ragged stone.

I feel made darker in the brightness of the sun,
things illumined that used to turn to gold

in broadest blue, and be a part of my earlier self.
That too returns from the summer's air,

like a hallucination, come to gaze in the corner
of the eye. A sudden rolling of sea-clouds

in the sinking green, a groaning thunder past
the threatening livid beam of wonder.

October Wind

It makes no difference, dear,
whether you sit here or there:
If I sit here and you sit
there, home is anywhere
our thoughts have roamed together.

It makes a difference, dear,
if in your dreams I hear
you call out my name or hers
when we are sleeping together
and I am left, trembling with fear.

It's so much safer, dear, if we
bear our burdens along separate
trails, alone, as all the way
from here to there
we can only rise.

Beneath A Dew

In the wearier air of November,
The old light moved from solid rock
To the weaker stones around it.
My soul could shrink into a shelter
Of leaves, rotted and fallen,
Touched by frost and a quieter dream.

In from the earth you came, to make me
A part of all things, to sing me
And shake me, ampler than the wind.
Over our bare spaces you call me in,
You, the bearer of a sky
That does not sting.

I am for you the woman in moonshine,
Bearing the scent of autumn weeds,
The pungent roots of other pasts,
Belonging to that wandering me.
A most tranquil thought, a total
Grandeur, thrills the chords.

Now the blushing sunset slides
From voluptuous mountain flanks.
The white-domed rooms forge
No regrets: a window view,
A simple desk, can still fulfill my
Rose-lit world.

"Whose world" are we to claim as our own,
Where green leaves came and covered
Stone, where lilacs came
And bloomed so bright that out of this light
The boundaries grow larger still?
No more than a bird-nest on a wing.

Leaving the Black Wound There

It was growing, spreading an actual
warmth behind my mind,
a passing link
encaged by words and
tugged by time.

In winter folds I kept it
warm, tearing
thoughts to petal-
shreds whose sadness moved
each
slowly
for each tear unshed.

During those colder days
seeking ways to secure
something made, a butter-
fly in shrinking hands,
I held death
to my breast
like an amulet.

I fear some music and
my mind, waiting,
as I recall tall moons,
in the slow dance
backwards to that time
his ashes flew
into the hungry
mouths of wind.

Only in Darkness

From the cold stone you have risen,
in a unique sound, bathed
in the slender rays of a white
winter sun.
You have shed your glorious skin
after mating stars
with purple rings. The wind-glass
has shattered all your
triumphs;
your mind has departed.
The bowl of water left outside
has frozen
and the bird has sung its song.
Only in darkness can you begrudge
those who have wronged you.

Winged

In the transmutation
reborn

you open
your

daring
wing

day
after
day
still

aspiring
to

a word:

"I
hear you!"

IV. Trespassing

As We Die

we die together
in our sleep –
5 p.m. Madrid.

As the bull in the red
we die – the love &
each barb held proudly.

Shall I wake as a seed
and you – as a bird
that sails above me?

Or have I maimed
the wing, as I aimed
at the eye to catch me?

Knowing not how deep,
I dig my teeth
into my own heart.

Still, the unleashed spirit
ties us together,
in this small space for breath.

An Age Away

There is a fear I feel whenever I write you,
more often than when, as I usually do, I speak aloud.

There are two paths at a right angle leading from
the steps to the garden. Between them stand

two plum trees wrapped about each other,
like the middle finger wrapped around the index,

their branches covering both path and steps.
No longer will I sit there telling you the tale

but will quietly ask myself, "What is it you fear?
Is it her voice when she answers? Is it her eyes

when she sees? Her anger...her smile...her tear?"
...Yes, each one but something plainer...

perhaps it's not fear at all but the simple fact
that you are not here. At times it hits me

with a sudden force, as if it had never
been understood before, as if I had woken

to find you gone.
Your letters come, as predictable as the doves –

one veers
and they all veer...

Absence

Mistress no more, the woman of grief,
lulled by crowns of summer leaves.
Ravenous roses in their second flush—but
no lover to leave her torn,
nor any grand finale, heaving her soul,
throbbing for more...

Down the fragrant path,
a bumble-bee crawls up a thistle head
and sails away in the drowsy air.
She might be desolate, abandoned, forlorn,
as she lies on the warm cracked stone
where they had first lain.
She is a dandelion gone to seed, long after
the harsh winds came
and shattered, like droplets of blood, the poppies' red.
She carries longings that slice her breast
and sweet swirls of torments.
Drawn by the soft light ahead
she is more than this empty shell:
A shadow tears through her
as she welcomes his absence instead.

Trespassing

I think of how you
dream our dream
and make the shadow glow
with a red darkness.
Behind the red
I move my offerings
closer to you,
my mind kept small.
You ask me not to bring
flowers,
your barren bed
close to the window,
where flowers dot
the ragged path.
You ask me to bring
my smile only,
my soft red lips
to comfort yours.
Yet I am but a black-hooded nun
as my lips whisper rhymes
to a God I cannot see.

Eternally

So close to insanity I feel
as close as I can come

to anyone but me even my
feet are on their own

scraping the grey tiles
of the waiting room.

Breathe. Don't stare. Don't
giggle. Don't chew a hundred

times. You are safe. I tell him
of the two doves. Pure-white.

One flew in the open space, the
other clung to the wall—a sign

or an answer to his question?
His eyes don't look away.

I envy the calm blue,
my head full of drafts and

banging windows, a million bits
of glass like lace around a bride's

face. Another burst of rain carries
a symbol. Open your wing-like

mouth. Speak to me. Dip from
your sky into my ruins so I can

find a way to enter light and
touch you as you draw near.

The Giant Room

I hear myself crying
but I'm not.
I am walking about
like a leprechaun
in a room full of goblins
and dusk
the fire burning,

but it is fake
Schumann,
real enough,
your newspaper
rustling,
the shadow of
your foot
to hold on to.

Earlier
the sun came up
as usual
but I mentioned
marriage—
"How appalling!"
you answered,
"How banal!"

Did you need a quarrel
so much, G., oh G.?
"Are you thinking of
someone else?"
I asked and you laughed
and called me TROLLE.

A Sky Not Seen by the Other

Not the ripe glow alone,
the universe of your eyes I kiss,
our ritual of the small morning
hours. Waves returning, spread,
unrolled overnight.

Deeper still
I've come to know you, your pale cheek.
Like a tired whale breathing clear space ahead
you send tiny bubbles up up up
and I fall, where you let go,
where I want more.

Was it wrong from the start?
A snapshot of the past, you
standing by the window thinking sea-
bones, just to preserve your identity.
So much hell it is to go against you.

Another time,
another life really to know.

The Wanting

I stand, in the doorway.
The light finds its shape in the cloud,
chafed at the edges.
The geese are gone. Their shrieks leave holes
in the air,
pellets of a hard substance.
Set close, the quiet dark craters of old habits.
So peaceful here where,
left dreamless,
I rub my back, I rub
the table clean of crumbs and circled smudges.

All this giving spills like hot milk,
leaving a dark crust.
It will crack like a dry wound
reopened, the burn up the shoulder, holding
the world with tears
until all the faith
wears out. I cannot bear this giving all at once.
I am heavy with giving,
afraid part of me will get lost on the cold floor,
with shreds of me swept into corners.
I need a broom shaped for me, the famished I,
to cut myself free from my addiction:
this piercing black tattoo—this wanting,
wanting you.

V. No Way Out

A Way Out

In a cheap hotel where the woman stays
to flee from never ending days,
she awaits her lover, leaving the door
to her room ajar
to hear his quiet footsteps on the stair.

But each time the front door opens
the man in number 14
calls out:
"Into the trenches!"
and she flees, as there is no way out.

Angels Lost

Down three flights men's voices
in a chorus rise upwards
to an attic with low beams
where the angels we lost
fit snug in a circle.

Our whispers hang in the warm air --
our words eluding, cracking,
choking, gliding
like nuggets
in a river's bed.

Hard pebbles in our mouths make us
falter, strenuously holding on
to the empty void
that needs to be filled.
Some breed rats,

some are afraid and toss their burdens
into a corner,
where a pious hunchbacked nun
will sweep them together,
a holy host for hungry winds.

Tea Time

Low across the face of the earth
old dreams walk in pairs.
The sheets are aired,
cushions fluffed,
a sky-coloured bed now shared with the cat.

The glorious waning sun cascades
from pillared windows --
irreproachable, the absence of gloom.
On winged feet, Messengers come
to the gilded room, to nibble and
mumble furry words,
a shoulder against the winter cold.
Cupping the ear with one hand,
while the other, slowly and firmly,
pours the tea.

Virginia's Bone Parlour

A torn piece of cloth covers her bones
at the bottom of a murky river,
like a flag around a sagging pole,
                                                                      yet
there was beauty there, where no one could see it.

Meandering for hours, the silent wail,
once young and angry,
                              now stepping on toes.
A man, a voice calling across an island,
always one dance step ahead
unbearably and provokingly dear.
Not meant to surrender the path to the river
that flows and forever sneers.
With curve and curl, the white knuckles of
her hands clutched at
                              those cold prison bars.
The call of an owl in the fallen night,
the fight for bright colours,
his love, longing for abundance,
for pride.

"Paint me real, I'll tell you my story,
yet I can't free you of yours."
Lulls and falls,
uncertainties, something growing
                              in the deep of sleep.
A dull sweet durance,
a frail move toward the next curve,
the straight line snapping
like a thread.
Remembering the best of peace
              she fills her pockets with rocks.

Poem Broken into Two Parts

I

Bamboo, shells, charts—
The swell of wind
In the landscape
Of your face

Bared teeth and fists
Against your Auden wall

I break away
And fall

II

...If not,
Silence again
Repeated
In the small space we needed
Then
To be angels
Before
We lived

Do You Still Care?

God feels...you understood,
but "Can't you see?" is what I asked
in the rainy felt morning.

You turned from me into your sleep.
Ours, the exhaustion, lived
anew.

The miracle of gold, cold and flesh.
As the curtain lightly moves,
your shoulder

is what I touch under the sheet.
From all the whispered
hesitations

I tremble away, and my question
flattens
against this precarious day.

This Paper Cage

Cold
the leafless bough, its spirit bending
to touch my face and fall over the old grey wall
ahead of me.
I wrap myself in a paper cage,
                    with a wildness like pleading—
and offer assorted toes and fingers
whenever you ask me to emerge.

So I tell myself, "Life is a passing sleep
                    but where will that waking be...?"
I watch the sun flirt and glow,
in its wintry mane,
before returning my shadow
back into the cage with me.

I know well my mountain's cold winds,
their calm and softening spell, the fields
of home.

Wearing bells, I'll paint my eyes
            for the journey and sing
with the only voice they gave me.

Under the Bough

Into a greater gift than words,
our silence scythes the clear evening.

I lay lavender to keep off the scorpions,
an apple against the other fruit rotting.

What candour under the bough?
The moon will wane but I can not change.

You are cleaning the fish tank, sucking out water
for a fish that belongs to no one.

I prefer the photographs on my walls
to talk to me, their stillness in time.

But before I end comes a hermit with weak hands
clenched against my sad and unused face.

Song of the Siren

Where would we be without death,
without seeking happiness
hereafter?
It is the quiet voice that speaks,
that makes us see the stars
when there are none.

Too old to be afraid, I know now
you are less real when I can't
hold you.
I won't be a house
filled by ghosts, if I can see...
I sing you here, I sing you now,
I know now I am less real
when you are not near.

When you walk into the night,
you reach for darkness,
toward that outer love:
Let me change my eyes and be
the green at the centre.
Like a lizard that keeps its tail,
I came not knowing something
could be taken.

The sun has gone above and over
the roof. All is fire and red,
under the cloak of sunset.
I will look for you with that singing
in my throat,
in the undertow that is beautiful.

A wave will snatch you from the cliffs
where you will remain, stranded,
a small distracted soul.
I am the lighthouse,
the siren,
my long hair covering my breasts.

VI. Back to the Earth with Feathers

Saving Snails

As I walk up the path when the sun is just rising,
A festival of snails with their perfect white shells
Meets me half way.

I will place little altars of serenity and grass
To aim them towards the open field, knowing that
By the time the sun is high,

As is their fate, they will be crushed by trespassers.

A Woman of Granted Roots

riding amber acorns wild
amid yellow autumn change,

easy folded browns that
waste in full perfection,

while warm and rotted underground
forest limbs are resting.

Golden bones of squirrels
gnawed by bare-teethed gnomes

unshackled virtues—violets and mint!
Nothing milky soft the armpit,

ripe the belly, chestnut hair a bridle
for zealous wintry winds.

White and greedy ermines on her shed:
voluptuous fur!

No knight to lift his sword or woo
a woman thus embalmed.

From the Cloud

She knew she would come back to earth with feathers,
flowing brilliant white
in a radiance of corn-flower's blue.
The cloud
alone, lit from within --
with no forceful wind
to drive
its triptych of color and glow.
A vendor of seeds
or a handsome toreador
might steal her heart, then ask for more
than she could give:

An opening of wings, a shattering!

Making This Heavy Rock a Place

There are no seams
to come
undone.
The rock is solid.
Rooted
trees and ivy leaves
curl
around gray stone,
throwing away
the light
of the moment
in its own flare.

The bird comes home
dragging its own
infinity
into the core
of the wall.
She sits behind
geraniums,
whiffs of jasmine
in mid air.

Beyond the last thought
a foreign song rises
from under the mountain.
The wind moves
slowly
in her forested mind.
It holds her true
to any man's
request, not another
weeping woman
pining for
death!

Bird of the Fall

Lay back,
bird of the fall.
Spread your bruised wing
and forget.

The little light is out
above the iron bed.
A lark's
two piercing notes
answer
the abysmal void

& cling to the cold lost embryo we were
long before we met
as brides of autumn.

This Is Joy

White tower against old mountains:
the sound of a horn as a sound of farewell,
serene, final...

White tower against shadowy night:
the mind washed out as the clean moon
across the sky...

White tower against wide open meadows:
Let me sleep on your lap and rest my cheek
in your open hand...

White tower against silvery mountains:
Throw about the light in a game of catch
without the madness of space...

White tower against sunset mountains:
In the soft, sunny vine weaving its stalks,
this blazing beam of joy is yours is mine...

Rose-Fish

Could I but let go of the years of peace that came before,
as a sailor must, passing foreign lands,
forget the shore—

watching the antics of a rose-fish deep down where no
sound
nor wind is heard, as a pearl
in the dark unstirred core—

had I followed the tiny paw prints in the sand,
not after the crying reached me
year after year—.

Have I shut my empty suitcase around an empty star,
adrift, aglow, and strong where
most fragile it is a star—

with lips as eager clap-traps nibbling at love, devoured
the stem, we live for the dead
who die if we die

but live, if we live, again.

The Borrowed Geranium

Summer 2008

The bird sings to the rich earth,
summer glittering made new,
consuming slender clouds.
Crickets orchestrate their hiding,
a welcome constancy.

On the steep path between apple trees
I follow you.
How can love be easier from afar?
Shafts of light cascading,
pristine vineyards sprawl
beneath the shadow.

Mountain ripples amber and stone,
a wilderness, growing within,
which no wall of hard rock can uphold.
Night moths cling to my curtains,
silent, and through the grape-leaves
the moon.

Granted a paradise humanly near,
unbearable the pain to forsake it
for something more dear,
the soul centred on a smaller life:
A greenness so tender in the tides
of the sun. Three pillars

on Confucius' mountain stand erect.
Swallows at dusk.
My song will be the nightingale,
tandaradei, a candle lit in the chapel,
to keep our loved ones.
Most frail, the pale glow, the armour
of leaves that shield the heart.

Daring Light

for Barbara

Amber swept away
by rivers of lava,
the seed is born
in the obscure womb
and the Valkyrie
intones her song.

The hand glows
slender and branded,
offering the present
its ample gift
of a solemn embrace—
overwhelming
and so often bitter.

Turgid and tenuous,
the shadow wanders
and flows
in amorous dances
(eternally restless)
that blur time,
an exiled body reborn
light and vain.

From the earth
the clear darkness,
from the grain
the heavy growing
arduous and filled
with hope—a gift
without deferring
fate—and a voluptuous
sigh.

The delicate zephyr
melts springs away.
You have gathered
spheres and brightened

souls, absorbed
in their secrets.

You are the tower
facing mine,
and between the two
we build a wake
diaphanous and
everlasting,
a bridge of pearls
that fade at sunset.
You
are the gleam of dawn.

The Wild Anemone

I'll call it the daring
flower its softness its

pallor so little suggesting
the strength with which

it fights the wind its
petals so delicate it

seems a touch would wither
them yet they'll outlast a

three-day storm and will
outlast I think [and now

I speak to her] the tempests
that a foolish heart invents

to plague itself because
it hardly dares to love

the wild anemone
the daring flower.

The Mask

Slithering ivy over the bronze mask
on the garden wall,
its leaves growing from my mouth
for words better left unsaid,
red in the autumn glow soon to be
winter dead.
Rain tears from hollow eyes
gliding on frozen cheeks
as memories hold on to rippled grooves,
the furrows of my face
thus buried before my time.
Seasons to torment the passing years,
seasons out of season,
fight the whirlpools of a rigid soul.
May your hand caress this cold bronze face
when I'm no more
and from a blue black sky
I'll shower you with stars and light—
one by one, to fill your heart
and linger on your brow,
seduced and replenished by etched shadows
falling falling inside you
like a golden bough.

Note by the Author

These poems were written on snippets of paper, long lost then found in old drawers or among stacks of paperwork. John Gery offered to look through them and make slight changes where he thought wise. I am very thankful to him for the time offered to this work.

As the title *Trespassing* suggests, I hesitated to pull them out of the closet, but as a siren's song they begged to be freed.

Further poetry works are *My Taishan* (Raffaelli Editore, 2007) in an English and Italian version, and *Dear Friends* (Palisade Press, 2008) with photographs by Lynda Smith. I am glad to report that *My Taishan* has been translated into Czech by the Czech poet and translator Petr Mikeš, published in April 2011. It is currently being translated into Spanish by poet Antonio Colinas and into Romanian. Biljana Obradovic has translated *Dear Friends* into Serbian, still to be published.

I'd like to dedicate these poems to my two sons, Demian and Cyril.

About the Poet

Patrizia de Rachewiltz grew up in the Tyrolean mountains of northern Italy. Born to a Russian-Italian father and an American mother, she is a multilingual poet, writer and translator. She was educated in Rome (French Baccalaureate) and Vienna. She has worked as a writer, translator, and language instructor. She has read her work at literary conferences in Italy and art galleries in Holland. She lives in 's-Hertogenbosch, the Netherlands, with her husband.

The Ezra Pound Center for Literature

The Ezra Pound Center for Literature Book Series is a project dedicated to publishing a variety of scholarly and literary works relevant to Ezra Pound and Modernism, including new critical monographs on Pound and/or other Modernists, scholarly studies related to Pound and his legacy, edited collections of essays, volumes of original poetry, reissued books of importance to Pound scholarship, translations, and other works.

Ezra Pound Center for Literature Book Series

The Imagist Poem: Modern Poetry in Miniature, William Pratt, Editor, (2008)

Trespassing, Patrizia de Rachewiltz, (2011)

I poeti di Sala Capizucchi/The Poets of the Sala Capizucchi, Caterina Ricciardi and John Gery, Editors, (2011)

Also Available from UNO PRESS

General Titles

**Sometimes Courage Looks Like Crazy: A Journalist's Story* by Kim Bondy, 978-1-60801-058-5 (2011)

Post-Katrina Brazucas: Brazilian Immigrants in New Orleans by Annie Gibson, 978-1-60801-070-7 (2011)

The Saratoga Collection, edited by Terrence Sanders, 978-1-60801-061-5 (2011)

**The Garden Path: The Miseducation of a City,* by Andre Perry, 978-1-60801-048-6 (2011)

Before (During) After: Louisiana Photographers Visual Reactions to Hurricane Katrina, edited by Elizabeth Kleinveld, 978-1-60801-023-3 (2010)

**Beyond the Islands* by Alicia Yánez Cossío, translated by Amalia Gladhart, 978-1-60801-043-1 (2010)

**Writer in Residence: Memoir of a Literary Translator* by Mark Spitzer, 978-1-60801-020-2 (2010)

**The Fox's Window* by Naoko Awa, translated by Toshiya Kamei, 978-1-60801-006-6 (2010)

Black Santa by Jamie Bernstein, 978-1-60801-022-6 (2010)

Dream-crowned (Traumgekrönt) by Rainer Maria Rilke, translated by Lorne Mook, 978-1-60801-041-7 (2010)

**Voices Rising II: More Stories from the Katrina Narrative Project* edited by Rebeca Antoine, 978-0-9706190-8-2 (2010)

**Rowing to Sweden: Essays on Faith, Love, Politics, and Movies* by Fredrick Barton, 978-1-60801-001-1 (2010)

Dogs in My Life: The New Orleans Photographs of John Tibule Mendes, 978-1-60801-005-9 (2010)

New Orleans: The Underground Guide by Michael Patrick Welch & Alison Fensterstock, 978-1-60801-019-6 (2010)

Understanding the Music Business: A Comprehensive View edited by Harmon Greenblatt & Irwin Steinberg, 978-1-60801-004-2 (2010)

**The Gravedigger* by Rob Magnuson Smith, 978-1-60801-010-3 (2010)

Portraits: Photographs in New Orleans 1998-2009 by Jonathan Traviesa, 978-0-9706190-5-1 (2009)

**I hope it's not over, and good-by: Selected Poems of Everette Maddox* by Everette Maddox, 978-1-60801-000-4 (2009)

Theoretical Killings: Essays & Accidents by Steven Church, 978-0-9706190-6-8 (2009)

**Voices Rising: Stories from the Katrina Narrative Project* edited by Rebeca Antoine, 978-0-9728143-6-2 (2008)

On Higher Ground: The University of New Orleans at Fifty by Dr. Robert Dupont, 978-0-9728143-5-5 (2008)

The Change Cycle Handbook by Will Lannes, 978-0-9728143-9-3 (2008)

Us Four Plus Four: Eight Russian Poets Conversing translated by Don Mager, 978-0-9706190-4-4 (2008)

The El Cholo Feeling Passes by Fredrick Barton, 978-0-9728143-2-4 (2003)

A House Divided by Fredrick Barton, 978-0-9728143-1-7 (2003)

William Christenberry: Art & Family by J. Richard Gruber, 978-0-9706190-0-6 (2000)

The Neighborhood Story Project

New Orleans in 19 Movements by Thurgood Marshall Early College High School, 978-1-60801-069-1 (2011)

The Combination by Ashley Nelson, 978-1-60801-055-4 (2010)

The House of Dance and Feathers: A Museum by Ronald W. Lewis by Rachel Breunlin & Ronald W. Lewis, 978-0-9706190-7-5 (2009)

Beyond the Bricks by Daron Crawford & Pernell Russell, 978-1-60801-016-5 (2010)

Aunt Alice Vs. Bob Marley by Kareem Kennedy, 978-1-60801-013-4 (2010)

Signed, The President by Kenneth Phillips, 978-1-60801-015-8 (2010)

Houses of Beauty: From Englishtown to the Seventh Ward by Susan Henry, 978-1-60801-014-1 (2010)

Coming Out the Door for the Ninth Ward edited by Rachel Breunlin, 978-0-9706190-9-9 (2006)

Cornerstones: Celebrating the Everyday Monuments & Gathering Places of New Orleans edited by Rachel Breunlin, 978-0-9706190-3-7 (2008)

The Engaged Writes Series

Medea and Her War Machines by Ioan Flora, translated by Adam J. Sorkin, 978-1-60801-067-7 (2011)

Together by Julius Chingono and John Eppel, 978-1-60801-049-3 (2011)

Vegetal Sex (O Sexo Vegetal) by Sergio Medeiros, translated by Raymond L.Bianchi, 978-1-60801-046-2 (2010)

**Wounded Days (Los Días Heridos)* by Leticia Luna, translated by Toshiya Kamei, 978-1-60801-042-4 (2010)

When the Water Came: Evacuees of Hurricane Katrina by Cynthia Hogue & Rebecca Ross, 978-1-60801-012-7 (2010)

**A Passenger from the West* by Nabile Farès, translated by Peter Thompson, 978-1-60801-008-0 (2010)

**Everybody Knows What Time It Is* by Reginald Martin, 978-1-60801-011-0 (2010)

**Green Fields: Crime, Punishment, & a Boyhood Between* by Bob Cowser, Jr., 978-1-60801-018-9 (2010)

**Open Correspondence: An Epistolary Dialogue* by Abdelkébir Khatibi and Rita El Khayat, translated by Safoi Babana-Hampton, Valérie K. Orlando, Mary Vogl, 978-1-60801-021-9 (2010)

Gravestones (Lápidas) by Antonio Gamoneda, translated by Donald Wellman, 978-1-60801-002-8 (2009)

Hearing Your Story: Songs of History and Life for Sand Roses by Nabile Farès translated by Peter Thompson, 978-0-9728143-7-9 (2008)

The Katrina Papers: A Journal of Trauma and Recovery by Jerry W. Ward, Jr., 978-0-9728143-3-1 (2008)

Contemporary Poetry

California Redemption Values by Kevin Opstedal, 978-1-60801-066-0 (2011)

Atlanta Poets Group Anthology: The Lattice Inside by Atlanta Poets Group, 978-1-60801-064-6 (2011)

Makebelieve by Caitlin Scholl, 978-1-60801-056-1 (2011)

Dear Oxygen: New and Selected Poems by Lewis MacAdams, edited by Kevin Opstedal, 978-1-60801-059-2 (2011)

Only More So by Tony Lopez, 978-1-60801-057-8 (2011)

Enridged by Brian Richards, 978-1-60801-047-9 (2011)

A Gallery of Ghosts by John Gery, 978-0-9728143-4-8 (2008)

The Ezra Pound Center for Literature

The Poets of the Sala Capizucchi (I Poeti della Sala Capizucchi) edited by Caterina Ricciardi and John Gery, 978-1-60801-068-4 (2011)

Trespassing, by Patrizia de Rachewiltz, 978-1-60801-060-8 (2011)

**The Imagist Poem: Modern Poetry in Miniature* edited by William Pratt, 978-0-9728143-8-6 (2008)

Contemporary Austrian Studies

Global Austria: Austria's Place in Europe and the World, Günter Bischof, Fritz Plasser (Eds.), Alexander Smith, Guest Editor, 978-1-60801-062-2 (2011)

From Empire to Republic: Post-World-War-I Austria Volume 19 edited by Günter Bischof, Fritz Plasser and Peter Berger, 978-1-60801-025-7 (2010)

The Schüssel Era in Austria Volume 18 edited by Günter Bischof & Fritz Plasser, 978-1-60801-009-7 (2009)

*Also available as E-book